UNIDENTIFIED FLYING OBJECTS YEARS 1290 - 2019

Written By Wayne Adams

Layout By Wayne Adams

Published by LuLu Books

ISBN: 978-1-67811-121-2

About the Author:
Wayne Adams graduated at Haskell University in 2009 with a Liberal Arts Degree and studied Meteorology. Wayne is currently a junior at Unity College studying a Bachelor's Degree in Environmental Science with emphasis in Climate Science. He has had many books sold on Amazon and Goodreads. This book was ranked in his top ten on Amazon for three months.

Introduction: This book looks at Unidentified Flying Objects and what they could possibly be. Many reports of UFOs from 1290 - present day. A look into the watchers and who they are? All of this will be answered in this book and more!

Chapter One Watchers

Holy watchers are angels sent by God to watch the movement and motives of humans on earth. They are to give an account to God of these such actions. The holy watcher can also give messages. Holy watchers can come in dreams or in waking life. We can find the first account of a holy watcher in Daniel 4 verses 10 - 11...10 I saw in the vision of my head upon my bed, and behold a watcher, and a holy one came down from heaven. 11 He cried aloud, and said thus: Cut down the tree, and chop off the branches thereof: shake off its leaves, and scatter its fruits: let the beasts fly away that are under it, and the birds from its branches. 12 Nevertheless, leave the stump of its roots in the earth, and let it be tied with a band of iron and of brass, among the grass, that is without, and let it be wet with the dew of heaven, and let its portion be with the wild beasts in the grass of the earth. 13 Let his heart be changed from man's, and let a beast's heart be given him: and let seven times pass over him. 14 This is the decree by the sentence of the watchers, and the word and demand of the holy ones: till the living know, that the most High ruleth in the kingdom of men: and he will give it to whomsoever it shall please him, and he will appoint the basest man over it. Holy Bible KJV pg. 513)

Unholy watchers are mentioned in the Bible as well, having sex with women producing men of great renown. Genesis Chapter 6: 1 And after that men began to be multiplied upon the earth, and daughters were born to them, 2 The sons of God seeing the daughters of men, that they were fair, took to themselves wives of all which they chose. (Holy Bible pg. 8) Job 1:6 Now on a certain day, when the sons of God came to stand before the Lord, Satan also was present among them. (Holy Bible pg. 639) Genesis 6:4 Now giants were upon the earth in those days. For after the sons of God went in to the daughters of men, and they brought forth children, these are the mighty men of old, men of renown. (Holy Bible pg. 8)

Chapter Two
Watchers Mentioned in Hindu

Ramayana is scripture taken out of the Hindu Holy Word. In this scripture, it talks about Vishnu one of their Holy deities focuses on aircraft that could fly and anything of that nature was not possible at the time. (UFO For The millions pg. 36 - 37) This could indicate that Vishnu was actually a holy or unholy watcher mentioned in the Bible?

Chapter Three UFO Reports 1290 - 1899

1290 in Yorkshire England a manuscript indicated a ufo had been observed by Henry Abbott. He was in the process of asking the blessing for his dinner when his brother came crashing through the door; screaming about a light in the sky. They all ran outside to see a silver disc
and it scared the wits out of them.
1490 in Ireland a silver disc came over a church during morning services. It scared the people very much and caused some sort of trembling; enough to cause a bell to fall.
In the late 1500s, an Italian church reported seeing silver discs in the sky. It was not mentioned if they felt it was

some sort of religious message being sent by angels.
Also, a titular object was noticed in the sky over Scotland
about the same chronological time frame.

In 1619, a luminosity entity was seen near a basin in
Fluelen Switzerland. Also, in 1644 a Spanish ship reported
seeing objects fly across the sky and foxtrot across up and
down in the heavens.

Florence, Italy reported December 9, 1731 orbs of glimmer
in the heavens. In 1755 terror was brought upon the city of
Lisbon, Portugal. Orbs of glimmer appeared there as well
foxtrotting in the heavens. Basel and Sole, Switzerland
astronomers reported axle pattern objects moving at
impossible intersections on August 9, 1762.

1816 Tottenham, England reported sparkling illuminations
in the sky. Also, in 1816 Lisbon, Portugal reported more
illuminations in the heavens; Edinburgh Scotland observed
a convex type pattern passing through the heavens.
Embrun, France observed on three abstract times aerial
phenomena making expeditious turns of 90-degrees. The
objects swooped away as fast as they appeared. In 1833
an enmesh forged object lingering in the heavens. A few
months later in 1833, a flying object with lights caught
people's attention in Niagara Falls, New York. 1836 a
mothership is seen shaped like a donut whirling on its own
support. In 1846 a ufo dropped jelly-like substance in
Lowell, Mass. The substance weighed 442 pounds and

four feet in diameter but no one understands what it is. 1849 an astronomer in France witnesses thousands of illuminated objects across the heavens. 1870 Lady of the Lake ship is at sea when the crew notices the bottom end of an oblique object branched into four fragments engulfed in a dust ball. July 6, 1874, Mexico residents observed a 400-foot object embodied as a trumpet, lingering in the heavens for six minutes. 1895 the ship H.M.S. Caroline was dispatched from Shanghai to Japan to observe disc-shaped objects in the heavens for two hours. The disc-shaped objects had a red enamel and cast-out brown chemtrails. San Rafel/San Francisco, California observes saucer-shaped discs illuminating over these cities in 1896. March 29, 1897, Omaha, Nebraska observed all across the city "a big bright light" blazing unwavering over the city then finally it went behind the houses of the horizon never to be seen again. March 30, 1897, a report from Decatur, Michigan said an airship similar to the reports in Omaha came over their city illuminating the ground. Human voices could be heard coming out of the object. April 9, 1897, more reports came in of an egg-shaped craft with illumination from Illinois to Wisconsin. On April 17 - 18, 1897, Iowa and Texas begin to report sightings of ufo demeanor. April 16 reports from Washington D.C. of flying objects over the city. The craft was 600 feet off the ground and flew toward the Washington Monument sailing off toward Georgetown before going out of sight. The objects were visible for ten minutes. April 22, 1897, Jim Hooten was near Texarkana, Arkansas and as a train engineer. He had a layover and went hunting. When Jim finished hunting he was on his way back to the train depot hearing a sound he decided to investigate. What Jim saw took him by surprise as it looked like a silo set on end. He met the occupants within the ship and spoke to them. The occupants of the ship told him they used "condensed air" to maneuver the ship. Then the people whom Jim Hooten met, boarded the ship, and headed for the heavens

.

Chapter Four
UFO Reports 1900 - 1952

In 1907 Burlington Vermont reported a torpedo

like craft over the city illuminating the

heavens with fire. The torpedo-like craft began to change color as it moved away from the city. Then a smaller disc like craft came out of the torpedo and they both

disappeared. January 1 - 4 a white craft flew over the city of Chattanooga, Tennessee and approached the city from a new direction each time it flew over. September 21, 1910 a million people saw a large number of ufos fly over New York City for three hours holding up traffic as people looked up to see the event. In 1915 a cigar shaped craft was reported from Huntington West Virginia. North Carolina reported UFOs (discs and bright objects) from 1920 to 1923. August 29, 1929, four hundred miles off the Virginia coast, a steamship observed a light in the sky. The light was traveling at estimated speeds of up to 100 miles per hour. (UFO For The millions pg. 36 - 48) From 1939 to 1945 the United States, USSR, Germany, Japan and all other countries reported strange lights in the sky. The United States Air Force called them

foo-fighters. Foo-fighters at the time in World War Two were thought to be German secret weapons by the United States military. Germans thought they were United States military secret weapons. Neither were correct as the foo-fighters were watcher angels observing the war. In 1947 the war was over and people forgot about the foo-fighters. A businessman named Frank Arnold was flying a private plane across Washington State when he noticed an illumination to his left. He saw nine disc shaped objects flying at 9500 feet by Mount Rainier . The disc shaped objects were skipping a long at high speeds of 1657 miles per hour. On June 28, 1947, Airforce pilots in Nevada and Alabama observed flying discs. On January 7, 1948 a tremendous number of people called the Kentucky Highway Patrol reporting a huge silver disc, Air National Guard was dispatched and pilot Captain Thomas Mantell took chase after the object. Mantell chased the object straight up to 25,000 feet with no oxygen in his plane . The Air National Guard ordered Mantell to come back but there was no answer. Mantell had run out of oxygen and his plane crashed back to earth. There Is still an argument today if Mantell was shot down by a UFO, or ran out of oxygen from chasing a weather balloon that was over Kentucky at the time. In 1948 two Eastern Airlines pilots, and people on the ground saw a cigar-shaped craft in the heavens. Between 1949 and 1951 UFO reports were scarce.

Chapter Five
UFO Reports 1952 - 1969 Project Blue Book

1952 was an amazing year for Unidentified Flying object reports. The Air Force received 1500 reports of UFOs.

Project Blue Book   (PBB) was developed as a secret UFO case study by the Air Force. The United States Government made a law that if anyone within PBB gave out information about UFO reports it was considered espionage and ten years in prison or a 10,000 dollar fine would be instituted. 1953 - 1969 PBB gathered tremendous amounts of reports on UFOs and investigated them. The final result was many of the reports could be identified as atmospheric anomalies. However, it was those little pieces, cases that they could not explain leaving PBB with questions that were never answered. (UFO's pg. 11 - 20)

Chapter Six
UFO Reports 1970 - 2017

1972 a man in Eastern Cape, South Africa saw a metallic style ball in the air that could not be explained at approximately 59,000 feet. Not long after the first report fifty factory workers reported the incident as well. The metallic ball was rotating and foxtrotting rapidly. The military of South Africa sent a jet after the object but the pilot could not locate the UFO. In 1976 a UFO was reported in Tehran, Iran. Two Iranian Air Force jets were sent by the Iranian military to chase after lights in the sky. Upon approaching the UFO all instrumentation within the jets ceased. When the Iranian jets withdrew from the craft all instrumentation began to work again. On October 21, 1978 an Australian pilot Fredrick Valentich disappeared over Bass Strait in his last radio transmission; it could be heard he had seen a UFO. He said the UFO was 1000 feet above his plane and then he said, "it is not an aircraft." Then his transmission was interrupted by metallic scraping sounds. The UFO had been toying with him before the final incident "playing chicken" if you will at his plane according to Fredrick in the air traffic control radio file report. However, air traffic control could not see anything on radar to confirm Fredrick's story. He was never heard from again. August 21, 1978, Safe Air Freight in New Zealand plane reported lights that followed then in their journey and was recorded by a TV crew on the ground. August 27, 1979, a Marshall County Minnesota Deputy Sheriff reported a bright light had hit his patrol car causing damage. The officer also reported eye retina damage from the bright light as well. November 11, 1979, a Spanish commercial airplane was forced to land because of a UFO. Red lights had been coming right at the commercial jet with 109 people on board. The pilot was afraid and decided to land the plane in order to avoid more contact with this set of lights. The air force in Spain sent a jet after the object. Not long after this military radar indicated three unknown objects that were 200 meters in length. One of the objects did a flyover of the airport runway. The military jet chased the object but had its systems jammed by the UFO. However, the pilot did get close enough to describe the object and said it looked like a cone.

April 11, 1980, a Peru fighter pilot fired 64, 30 mm shells, at what appeared to be a lightbulb in the sky. The pilot never could make contact with any of the shells and the lightbulb in the sky disappeared. November 17, 1986, a Japan commercial jet was flying over Alaska and reported a square craft not long afterwards air traffic control also was able to pick it up on radar following the commercial jet.

March 30 - 31, 1990, Belgium military radar indicated two unknown crafts and sent military aircraft to search for them which turned up nothing. 143 people reported seeing

triangles in the sky .

October 5, 1996, a private pilot saw a cone UFO as big as a soccer stadium. Also, military radar indicated the object as well to confirm the pilot's story. The private pilot flew around the object for 15 minutes before it flew off toward the sea. March 13, 1997, thousands of people from the Nevada line to past Phoenix Arizona to Tucson reported seeing a V shaped large object in the sky with lights. This incident is called "Phoenix Lights". The Governor of Arizona in 1997 Fife Symington actually witnessed the UFO sighting and said it was "otherworldly". He said it was about the size of an aircraft carrier.

November 11, 2004, Commander David and Lt. Commander Jim Strait was on a US military jet training mission, when a controller from the USS Nimitz reported a UFO near their location. The two commanders went to inspect what the controller had seen. When approaching the area a tic tac type object was observed foxtrotting then moving away with extreme speeds. USS Princeton picked it up on their ship radar. November 7, 2006, civilian, United Airlines employees and pilots saw a saucer-like craft

hovering over Chicago O'Hare airport. Then with the speed of non-human possibilities took off straight up out of sight. April 23, 2007, a commercial airliner over or near Alderney Island. The pilot and passengers observed two unidentified aircraft for ten to fifteen minutes. Air traffic control radar also picked up two objects to confirm their story. The UFO had a yellow light and looked like a cigar with a band wrapped around it. January 1, 2008, a UFO was picked up on radar near Stephenville, Texas by air traffic control. In the process of the event a private pilot witnessed the UFO and said it is about half a mile wide and a mile long. This sighting was so publicized by the media even "Larry King Live" at the time did a story on this UFO sighting. June 8, 2008, a police helicopter over the Bristol Channel, United Kingdom chased a black triangle UFO. The police helicopter chased the black triangle from Bristol Channel to Sully, United Kingdom. January 25, 2010, many citizens in Harbour Mille NewFoundland reported lights in the sky. A few days later Canada Government said it was a missile launch but not long after retracted the missile launch explanation. July 12, 2013, a black triangle was seen over the West Midlands of the United Kingdom by a commercial airline. The pilots saw this thing approaching their cockpit and did not have time for an evasive maneuver. The pilots ducked as they thought the black triangle would crash into the plane but was gone when they realized it had missed. The news called this sighting the Dudley Dorito. June 4, 2014, John Sheppard while putting out a bonfire saw lights in the sky over the Gulf of St. Lawrence. Mr. Sheppard recorded the event for twenty-two minutes. 2014 The Chilean government released a video of an unidentified flying object from a military helicopter. The UFO hovered for a bit before releasing some sort of gaseous substance or liquid then quickly went up into the clouds. The UFO seemed to be a black bale almost like a giant square bale of hay. 2015 off the east coast from Virginia to Florida in the USA. Two Navy pilots observed a craft of unknown origin on their targeting system of a Hornet fighter jet. 2017 in the skies over Arizona a commercial airline jet reported something passing above them at 3000 feet. Air traffic control could not see it on radar.

Chapter Seven
World Governments Take on UFO Phenomenon

Former United States Defense employee Luis Elazondo claims the government does indeed investigate UFO sightings. He has started a business where people come to him bringing supposed UFO materials to be tested. Great Britain as well has done investigations in the UFO phenomenon. Mr. Pope was a journalist hired by the British Government to investigate reports of UFOs. He has knowledge that many UFOs almost hit commercial airliners or caused interruption in the commercial airline traffic taking evasive action from time to time. He claims that there is a serious national security issue with UFOs. He claims that Russia, China, and other countries were investigating UFOs as well. Nick Pope says that some of the UFO reports could be aircraft made by Russia or China. https://www.youtube.com/watch?v=1ruFixSu0wA

Chapter Eight
Alien Abduction 1961

Betty and Barney Hill were reported to have been abducted by aliens September 19, 1961. Betty and Barney Hill were from Portsmouth, New Hampshire and decided to make a trip to Niagara Falls, New York September 19, 1961. Barney was a mail sorter for the United States Post Office in Boston which was a 120 mile trip daily. Betty was a social worker for the state of New Hampshire. They made it to Niagara Falls, New York spending a fine day there. On their way back a hurricane was brewing along the east coast so they decided to go home through Canada instead of dealing with the potential winds and rain of the storm. This new track sent them through Montreal, Canada. At around 9 P.M. they crossed the border, stopping to eat at a little place called Coleman, New Hampshire, along State Highway 3. They continued south along US Highway 3 to near Lancaster, New Hampshire; where they observed a glossy illumination near the moon. Barney deliberated it must be a satellite off course. However, the illumination suggested it was staying up with them. Barney after looking through binoculars thought it might be an airplane. Betty peered through the binoculars and found it to be a large UFO with fenestrations. In all of the excitement they had veered off

US. Highway 3. Barney realized the light had come down to tree height. He decided to stop the car and walk out into a field with the binoculars, coming within fifty feet of the illumination. Barney realized it was an object that resembled a flapjack with fenestrations. He also noticed a few incumbents within the craft. They appeared to be dressed in "Nazi-style uniforms". Barney ran in horror for consternation he would be apprehended. He sped off in the car with Betty in a raging panic. Then all of a sudden as they rushed down the road could hear a summoning sound in the rear of the vehicle. That is all they could remember when waking up near Ashland, New Hampshire on US Highway 3. Then they heard another introduction of summons as they drove down US Highway 3 toward Portsmouth, New Hampshire. When the Hills made it home they noticed some polished discoloration on their car. Also, they noticed a compass needle waving recklessly. The Hills then reported the incident to the Pease Air Force base. Within a seven day period she had dreams of unholy watcher angels leading them onto a craft and studying their bodies for medical purposes. Later, Barney consummated their trip took two hours more than it should in a normal situation. In this time frame the unholy watcher angle had taken them in the spaceship and observed their bodies in a medical observation.

The unholy watcher angels when speaking with Betty on the ship could not idealize what aging and time was. This is because unholy watcher angels are from a part of another dimension that does not require time or aging. They have no knowledge of these concepts. Radar from Pease Air Force Base had exhibited an unexplained return, where the Hills claimed they were abducted during this time frame. This is the best case that could have come through Project Blue Book! It proved unholy watcher angel abduction (Genesis 6:4) as in the Bible but a psychologist at the time dismissed it as a dream and nothing more. (Alien Abductions pg. 11 - 17)

Chapter Nine
The Book of Enoch and Watcher Angels

The Book of Enoch was rejected by the Jewish Sanhedrin because it gave prophecies of Jesus Christ. Early church fathers believed the book of Enoch to be inspired by the Hand of God. Most Christian churches today have rejected the book of Enoch. However, the Christian Ethiopian Orthodox Tewahedo Church still has the Book of Enoch in its cannon. Regardless, we peer into the book of Enoch for some answers to who the unholy watchers are. In Genesis 6:4 the Bible says that the sons of God (holy waters rebelled to unholy watchers) came down and had sex with then women of men producing men of great renown. One could find all kinds of examples from human books who the men of great renown were. I tend to believe it was the Greek Mythology examples. However, there is no proof to present a claim for any intention of accuracy. The watchers (what people today call aliens) had power over Enoch's people. Enoch said they were angels but could appear as men when they wished. These unholy watcher angels according to the book of Enoch took women as their wives as men do and had children. The unholy watcher angels in the Book of Enoch taught writing skills. Then the book of Enoch takes a turn toward modern day UFO stories. Enoch says he was taken up in a vehicle that could fly and uses a wall of hailstones to possibly mean he was looking through glass walls. Enoch said there were tongues of fire which could mean exhaust or something of that nature. Enoch says, God told the unholy watcher angels that because they rebelled with little knowledge, and never completed their education the knowledge was worthless. Their knowledge they had learned but not completed their education would lead to nasty consequences brought forth by God.

Chapter Ten
The Unholy Watchers Powers and Their Names

1. Unholy watcher angel Armaros educated the people on the process of witchcraft.
2. Unholy watcher angel Azazel taught humans how to form blades, art and cosmetics.
3. Unholy watcher angel Gadreel educated the people on archery and death fighting.
4. Unholy watcher angel Baraqel taught on horoscopes.
5. Unholy watcher angel Chazaqiel educated the people on weather forecasting.
6. Unholy watcher angel Kokabial taught horoscopes but also has 365,000 unholy watcher angels under his command.
7. Unholy watcher angel Penemue educated the people about writing with ink on paper.
8. Unholy watcher angel Sariel taught about the moon and how it orbited around the earth.
9. Unholy watcher angel Samyaza is the commander.
10. Unholy watcher angel Shamshiel educated the people about the sun and all of its power.

11. Unholy watcher angel Yeqon (also known as Lucifer possibly satan or the devil) he tempted the angels to fall and do his bidding.

Chapter 11
As In the Days of Noah

The bible says as in the Days of Noah so shall the days of the Son of Man be,...In the days of Noah there were holy watchers and unholy watchers. There was leviathan (a giant sea serpent) and giants. Today there are reports of leviathan like creatures in the sea and some in the lakes but no real evidence supports the claims except for pictures and word of mouth. Giants still roam the earth as in Andre the Giant (passed away) and the Big Show as they call him in the wrestling world. These men were and are seven foot or more tall. In the days of Noah evil was abundant and in today's world calamity gets worse every year. UFO reports as described by Enoch and today UFO reports as described in this book. It appears we are in the days Jesus Christ referred to as the last days. Yet is it upon us as the end of the world referred to in the Bible? I don't think we are that far along but each year we get closer. The temple has not been built back yet and the 12th Imam has not come. I believe many things are still undone including a war mentioned between the USA and Iran in Daniel 8. Either way, this book was written to suffice that UFOs are vehicles as written in Ezekial for angels to move around in and do their bidding. Unholy watcher angels use these vehicles to deceive humans into believing aliens exist, so, when the evil one comes they can trick the masses.